My Search For God

Bill Ferron

Copyright ©2013 Bill Ferron

Paperback ISBN: 978-0-9857060-2-9
e-book ISBN: 978-0-9857060-3-6

All rights reserved. No part of this publication may be reproduced, stored in or introduced into a retrial system, or transmitted in any form or by any means, electronic, mechanical, recording or otherwise, without the prior written permission of the author.

Printed in the United States.

First Edition

Book Cover

The photograph shown on the cover is an image of the Crab Nebula taken by the Hubble space telescope. A nebula, by definition, is a region of space where a vast cloud of gas (mostly hydrogen) is collapsing upon itself to form a new star. I think of this as one of the many places in our vast universe where one can find God actively at work as His creation continues to unfold.

My son, Bob Ferron, another of God's creations, designed the cover. One of his most precious gifts is the gift of creativity. His imagination and patience lead to beautiful finished products.

Table of Contents

Title Page
Copyright Information
Cover Design
Introduction
1. Faith Begins with a Simple Prayer
2. A Tough Reading Assignment
3. Easter Offers Us Hope
4. The Crazy Driver
5. Dad Teaches Me an Important Lesson
6. Message From Mary
7. How I Became the Absent Minded Professor
8. Prayer Answered
9. Crisis
10. The Importance of Relationships
11. A Close Call
12. Putting It All Together

Conclusion
Acknowledgement
References

Introduction

America and most the rest of the world are currently experiencing a crisis in faith. There are probably many factors contributing to the decline. The important thing is not to moan about how we got into this mess, but to correct the errors and thus reverse the trend. We can do this by rediscovering our relationship with God and by building loving relationships with the people He has placed on our paths.

This inspirational book is a chronological account of the twelve primary events that highlight my faith journey. I believe it can help to ease the crisis. Each of the twelve messages played a prominent role in shaping my faith. My journey begins with a simple prayer and includes at least one life changing event, a crisis and my own close call with death. Each of those experiences ultimately strengthened my faith

When I looked back upon those events or experiences, I discovered that each occurred at a crossroads in the development of my own faith. The most amazing thing was the realization that God was there to guide me when I asked for help. This does not mean He always chose to honor my requests. If He was there for me, there is no reason why He would not be there for you. All that seems to be required to build this relationship is a strong determination to find Him coupled with a positive outlook and optimistic attitude. Questions for reflection at the end of each chapter should help us to find our God and thus reconnect.

Robert Frost summarized the crux of the issue we must address when he stated "Two roads diverged in a wood, and I - I took the one less traveled by, and that has made all the difference..." We all must be willing to travel down the road less travelled in order to place the spotlight back on God.

If you let His image shine,
You will discover the divine.
Just seek Him and you will find Him
In the events of your own time.

1
Faith Begins with a Simple Prayer

My mother taught me a simple prayer when I was very young. It reads as follows:
> "Now I lay me down to sleep.
> I pray the Lord my soul to keep.
> If I should die before I wake
> I pray the Lord my soul to take."

I did not have a clue what a soul was or who the Lord might be, but the rhyme had a rhythm that was memorable and became a ritual every night after I was tucked under the covers of my bed.

I began to understand more about that prayer when I was five. This was when my younger brother and I first began to stay the occasional night with my grandmother. This was a special treat for us if we had been extra good during the week.

The first thing that my grandmother taught us was that our prayers should be said while kneeling beside the bed. One night she showed us how by kneeling beside us. We recited our little prayer and started to scramble up onto her big soft bed. We never got much more than our knees up on the bed before Grandma indicated that our prayers were not quite finished. She told us that we had not thanked the Lord that Mom and Dad let us stay with her or for the good meal we all enjoyed before Mom and Dad went home. So we hopped back down off the bed to finish our prayers.

The next time we stayed overnight with grandma we discovered who the Lord was. Grandma had a sick kit which she explained was used in the home for anointing people when they were very sick. The sacred heart of Jesus was the centerpiece of that kit. It showed just the head and a small portion of the chest of Jesus revealing a huge heart that was coming out of His chest. I naturally had to know why His heart was so big. Grandma explained to us that the Lord had to have an extra large heart because He had a lot of sick people to heal. That statue was my first exposure to the Lord who was the person in our prayer.

Sometime within the next two years my mother purchased two framed prints for our bedroom wall. The predominant color of the prints was blue. The artist was very good at capturing facial expressions in his pictures. One print showed the profile of a little boy kneeling beside his bed and saying his prayers while his mother watched. Her head was turned toward the viewer. She looked very pleased and happy. The second print showed the same little boy in the corner of his room because he had been bad. His dog was sitting on the floor and facing the boy, but the artist had drawn the head of the dog turned back toward the viewer once again. This time the dog looked so lonesome and forlorn because his playmate was being punished.

The looks on those two faces showed me the impact of good and bad on others. I knew from the first moment I saw those pictures that I wanted to be good and not bad and praying might be an important activity if I really wanted to be good.

Now, as I look back upon these events, I have come to realize that God often uses people and objects to shape our minds. Mom and Grandma were the people in this first story and the Sacred Heart of Jesus as well as the prints influenced my earliest steps as I began to journey along my path to God, but prayer opened the door. Faith really does begin with prayer.

Questions:
I told you the people, places and objects that God used as He began to forge a relationship with me. What were the people places and events that He used to begin building a relationship with you?
What is your favorite prayer or prayers?
Was your first faith recollection the day you first believed as stated in the song *"Amazing Grace"* or did it take a variety of people, places, objects and events before you first truly believed like it did with me?
Have you shared any of your thoughts about faith with family or friends?

2
A Tough Reading Assignment

My second grade teacher really focused on the importance of reading. I don't know exactly what she said, but I was ready, willing and eager to jump into something different than the three word sentences of my <u>Dick and Jane</u> reader.

I hurried home from school that afternoon and told Mom everything I knew about reading which was very little. I even told her that I did not want to see Dick run anymore since Dick was my little brother and I already knew that he could run very well.

Mom thought reading was a good idea so I began showing off my skills to her every evening after dinner. We began by reading familiar stories from some of my favorite books that she had read to me. It took only a few months to zip through most of the few books for children at our house. She told me that I sounded out unknown words quite well and that I no longer really needed her assistance.

One night I finished the last story in our collection of nursery rhymes for children and was ready for another book. When I mentioned it to Mom she told me that she would find something that would be good to read. I anxiously waited by my bed the next night wondering what that next book might be. Mom did not keep me waiting long. She arrived carrying a big book. She told me that this was an important book for adults, but it would give me lots of practice reading unfamiliar words. You will get stuck on many of them so I will help you figure out how to pronounce the difficult words. She explained that I should not worry if I did not understand some of the things that I read since very few adults really understood everything found in this book.

  The big book handed to me is called <u>The Bible</u>. It took me forever to read and she was right about my needing lots of help both with the words and with understanding, but I refused to throw in the towel and cry uncle. My persistence paid off as I eventually finished the final word on the last page. I had read this big book from cover to cover.

  What did I learn from this project? I am sorry to say that I learned only a small fraction of its message as I was only seven or eight years old at the time

Mom taught me that I might have learned more than I gave myself credit for as she asked me to tell her about some of my favorite Bible stories. When she asked me what my favorite story was, I told her that was easy. It was a story about a boy named David and a mean Philistine giant. The giant was covered with body armor and brandished a menacing sword. David had no armor and carried a sling and five rocks, but he slaughtered the giant with just one fling of his sling. She then reminded me that I had my own similar battle just a year earlier. There was a big bully who was pushing me around and taking food out of my lunch box. You asked dad what to do and he told you the next time he pushed you around or started to grab your lunch box, just drop it on the ground, jump on him and start swinging. You won that battle and ultimately became good friends which was an even better ending for a story.

She then asked me if I liked any of the other stories that I had read. I told her that I found several other stories exciting: The parting of the Red Sea by Moses, Noah and the Ark,

Jonah and the Whale, the adventures of Shadrach, Meshach and Abednego in the fiery furnace, as well as the miracle Jesus performed to bring His friend Lazarus back to life all captured the imagination of this young boy.

Now, when I reflect upon these experiences as an adult, I see one thread weaving all my favorite stories together. They taught me that the God to whom I prayed each night could do anything. That was all I captured from my first encounter with the Bible, but it was a really important insight. Yes, this was one really tough reading assignment. I grasped few of the many valuable lessons it presented, but my faith took another baby step forward that year. If He could do all those incredible things for those people, He could certainly help this young boy find his way in this crazy world

Questions:
When did you begin to wonder if there might be something or someone much bigger than us that first made this world possible then filled it with everything needed?

Have you ever read the Bible? It is the best place to learn more about that something or someone behind the scene pulling all the strings. I call that someone God.

Why does the Bible continue to be the most widely read book in the world?

Are the messages found in the Bible more relevant or less relevant to people today? Why?

3

Easter Offers Us Hope

It was a beautiful spring day during one of those many months that I had been working on my tough reading assignment. I did not have school since it was the last day of Easter Vacation. My brother and I had already pawed through our Easter baskets seeking out all the treasures hidden in the grass. We finished gobbling down a couple of bowls of cereal apiece and were getting ready to play out in what we considered to be our yard. It consisted of the two acres that belonged to dad and the two vacant acres on either side of us.

While we had all this space to play in, we chose to start our morning out by the dirt road that ran by our property. Both my brother and I liked this spot because it provided the only four foot high dirt bank anywhere in our yard. Our road had been cut through the surrounding countryside. Then a trench had been dug out on either side of the roadway to drain water off the surface of the road. The excess dirt from the roadway and trenching operations created this perfect embankment which made the ideal staging area for us to station our troops for battles with an imaginary enemy on the other side of the embankment.

This particular morning we decided to play war, so we each loaded up our small bucket with our armies (about twenty tiny plastic soldiers for the two of us to share, a couple of plastic tanks and jeeps and our own trenching equipment which was nothing more than two large old serving spoons along with a couple of worn table knives. We each dug out a new cave as a shelter for our troops and were in the midst of carving out a road linking our caves when something unusual happened. A family that was all dressed up was walking down the hill toward us. The man had on a dark suit and tie and the mother wore a pretty spring dress that was the same light blue color as her daughter's. They said hello as they passed us and continued down the hill. I watched them for a moment and then glanced back up the hill. There was another mom and dad coming down the hill. They were also all dressed up. I didn't notice what the mom and dad wore, but a little boy about the age of my brother had on a dark brown pair of pants and a white shirt. Their little girl was wearing a beautiful white dress that puffed way out from her legs as she skipped along in front of her family. I could see that her dress was bordered with pink flowers across the bottom edge of the dress as she came closer.

I ran in the house and asked mom what was going on just as they walked past our driveway. Mom glanced out the window in time to see the family heading down the hill. Then she looked down at me and said she thought they were going to the little white church at the bottom of the hill to celebrate Easter. I looked back up at her and blurted out without thinking "Why aren't we going there too?"

She said that was a very good question and then mentioned that she would talk to dad to see how he felt about the idea.

I now felt guilty about blurting out my question. I had learned from mom that dad had lost his mother when he was less than two years old and had never been to any church. I also learned from Grandma that my mother had been raised as a Catholic, but the whole family had stopped going to church when Grandma's husband died leaving them without transportation.

I would not be surprised if my parents never got around to talking about the request of a little boy who had no right to ask them to talk about a sensitive subject such as religion. I vowed to never mention that topic again.

I was shocked to discover two weeks later that we were heading down our hill to find out more about the little white church right after breakfast. It was a small friendly place named Trinity Presbyterian Church. We attended the church service followed by Sunday school for Dick and me. Mom and Dad socialized with the other Sunday school parents over coffee while we started learning more about the stories in the Bible.

The faith of our whole family took a giant leap forward that day. My brother and I were baptized at that church. We all attended church faithfully until we graduated from high school. Dad eventually became an elder and Mom was active in one of the women's church circles until the church finally closed its doors many years later.

I now often wonder what would have happened if it had not been such a beautiful day, if we had chosen to play in our back yard instead of out by the street, if those beautiful families had not chosen to walk instead of ride that day, and If I had not asked that fateful question.

I have no idea who either of those families was to this day, but they changed the lives of every member of our family. They were coming to share in an Easter celebration. We missed out on that celebration that year, but we have never missed another Easter celebration. Easter offers us eternal hope. I thank God for sending those families down our quiet rural road at just the right moment so we could share in that hope.

Questions:
This time God used two unknown families and a spontaneous question to solidify His relationship with our whole family. Who did He use to help solidify His relationship with you?
Can you recall the first time that you entered a church or synagogue or other place of worship?

Did that faith community strengthen your faith by helping you learn more about God?

4

The Crazy Driver

Each of the first three stories has contributed to my faith development. This story did not seem relevant to me at the time that it happened, but the more I thought about it, the more important it became. I share it with you because I am certain that every person reading this book has had a similar experience at one time or another in their own lives.

This story occurred in 1949 or 1950, back in the days before seat belt inclusion was an indispensable part of the safety equipment found in cars. Dad was driving us all home from one of our many trips to Grandma's house. Mom was sitting in the front passenger seat and my brother and I were in our usual positions in the back seat. Dick was behind Dad and I was behind Mom. Both of us were standing and I remember that I was holding onto the back of my mother's seat with both hands. It had been a pleasant day and all of us were happily chatting with one another as we neared home that evening.

Seventy second street marked the end of the city limits for Omaha and the last stoplight prior to home. We were facing west and sitting behind another car on Maple Street waiting for our light to turn from red to green. When it did, our line of traffic began to move. We were just beginning to pick up speed as we entered the intersection when Dad noticed another car barreling toward us travelling from the North at a high rate of speed. Dad knew instantly that he could not get across the street or stop the car in time to avoid a violent collision. He also knew that he could not turn across the line of cars that were coming from the other direction. Mom screamed and I fell down as He whipped the steering wheel hard to the right narrowly missing the crazy driver as he flew by us without even slowing. Then my dad whipped our car back to the left crossing behind him and driving into the ditch beside Maple Street. He had enough sense to keep the car moving so that we would not become mired in the ditch. He gradually pulled back onto the road once the way was clear. I thought the whole episode was an exciting new adventure until my dad started cursing. I noticed that he was red in the face and was trembling as he continued to curse all the way home. He had been visibly shaken and it did not get better as he began to inspect the car for damage after we were safely parked in our driveway. The damage seemed minor to me as the car escaped with nothing more serious than numerous paint scratches from some of the larger pieces of brush and roadside debris.

Dad was calmer the next morning, but his eyes were red. When I asked him why his eyes looked unusual, he told my brother and me that he did not get much sleep during the night. Then he sat us down and told us he estimated that the runaway car was travelling at a speed close to forty five miles an hour as it roared past us without ever slowing. Then he mentioned the probable outcome if we had been struck by someone travelling at such a high rate of speed. We would almost certainly have been seriously injured or killed. Suddenly what I had thought had been an exciting adventure the prior evening had been recast in a much more somber light. I finally realized that what had been an interesting departure from the normal drive home had been a horrifying experience for my parents.

Now, as I reflect back upon this incident, I realize that the shaking and cursing of my father during the rest of the drive home were behaviors associated with the adrenalin rush that accompanies the flight or fight response to extreme danger. I also realize the evasive steps my dad took that night were counter intuitive. A far more normal response would have been to turn away from the threat rather than into it. Nevertheless, my dad had responded in the only way possible to prevent the collision. Dad was always an excellent driver until he reached old age, but I sometimes wonder if God may have been guiding his hands on that particular evening. This could very well have been the end of my faith journey. I sense that at the very least, the journey would have been drastically altered. I now count this event as one of the many blessings in my life. This experience did nothing to strengthen my faith. It simply gave me the opportunity to continue my faith journey and God more time to strengthen His relationship with our family.

Questions:
What experiences, if any, lead you to believe that God may have saved your life at one time or another?
Who, other than you, was involved?
Have you thanked them?

5

Dad Teaches Me an Important Lesson

Have you noticed that it is impossible to reason with young children, or that words are inadequate to modify behavior? That was the case at my house at least and Dad was the designated enforcer when words fell short. A mild spanking that bruised our egos more than our behinds was his manner of discipline.

I was a typical older brother. My brother was about two and a half years younger than me so I naturally got to do everything first. I assume this was a very frustrating position for my brother as we grew older. The sad truth was that I added to his frustration with my own teasing behavior. This often led him to strike out in anger. Most of the time the anger was low key and led to nothing more than disputes which Mom handled by separating the two of us and giving us some chore or activity to get our minds on something other than our quarrel.

The teasing and bickering sometimes resumed when either of us was in a particularly feisty mood. On those days Mom would separate us, stand us in corners for five to ten minutes in different rooms and then warn us to expect a visit from the enforcer if she had to separate us again.

The warnings were usually sufficient to help us straighten up for the rest of the day in order to avoid additional discipline. Perhaps this was mom's way of letting us know that we only got three strikes before we were out. No arguing with the umpire was permitted. It also emphasized the point that it always takes two to tease, bicker or fight so we both would get our licking if we struck out at one another a third time. I am certain that the graded responses from Mom lessoned visits from the enforcer. However boys will be boys and sometimes we required additional discipline.

Dad worked most of his life at Paxton and Vierling Steel Company in Omaha, Nebraska. His job was to transform the information on blueprints directly to the steel so that girders and beams would join together to complete bridges and buildings. His work schedule was very consistent and we could count on him arriving home at 5:30PM on Monday through Friday and at 12:30PM on Saturday. We must have been particularly feisty one Saturday morning as we had already received our third strike and knew additional discipline was in our immediate future.

I must have been nine or ten years old at the time. I have no idea what we were arguing about, but I was not looking forward to the inevitable punishment when dad came home. I only remember that it had to be Saturday because our basement home faced east and there still was plenty of sunshine lighting up the face of my dad as he began to spank me. I remember the spanking well as what my dad said at that moment sounded so strange to my ears. His exact words were "This hurts me more than it hurts you." I thought to myself 'no way' as it was my bottom that was going to be red and not his tough hand. I looked back at him with my own tear filled eyes at the conclusion of my spanking just as the sun caught a tear streaming down his cheek. The radiance of his tear made a lasting impression on me. I believe God, Himself, was in that tear because the tear penetrated my heart creating a lasting impression.

I had never seen my dad shed a tear before or after that moment. Those words changed my behavior more than all my prior spankings combined. He taught me another meaning for love that day. I finally realized that my teasing hurt my brother; it angered and hurt my mother and it really did hurt my father in a way I would never completely understand until I became a parent many years later.

I definitely grew up a lot from this experience. I egged my brother on far less frequently. I am not certain, but I also believe that was the last time either of us received a visit from the enforcer.

The valuable lesson I learned was that the words I expressed in the first chapter about wanting to be good like the boy in the picture were meaningless if they were not accompanied by actions reinforcing the words in a loving manner. In other words, it was time for me to become less of a hypocrite.

Questions:

I am certain that you have your own experiences that helped you strive to be your best. Which ones helped you grow the most?

Do you agree that discipline helps to modify unacceptable behavior?

How do you distinguish between discipline and abuse?

Can you describe the last time when your words and the actions that ensued appeared to contradict one another?

I believe today that God was behind all the events described in previous chapters, but this was the first time I sensed the presence of God in the moment. What was the first memorable experience in your own life where you may have sensed His presence?

6

Message from Mary

I believe that everyone experiences life changing moments at times. The stories that I shared in the preceding chapters each contributed to my faith development. The ones that follow also helped to mold my character. The story presented in this chapter played the most pivotal role in shaping my faith as well as my future. It occurred during the winter of my senior year in high school.

This story began with a phone call From Doris, my latest girlfriend. We had been dating for about three months when I picked up the phone and said hello. The first words I heard were "We have to talk."

I thought this was what we were doing at that moment and just about every night of the week. When I asked her what she wanted to talk about, she said something like 'you don't understand, we really have to talk. Can you come over?'

This sounded serious so I said I would be there as soon as I could make it. I warned her that it would take me longer than normal because my car would not start due to the cold weather.

The phone call grew more and more ominous as I began to ponder the strange words that greeted my ear when I had picked up the phone ten minutes earlier. By the time I completed the mile and a half walk from our rural home to the bus stop, I was pretty sure that our relationship was about to end. I was certain I was getting the axe by the time I arrived at her home.

Doris greeted me at the door with a pleasant enough smile, but the serious talk began as soon as I removed the hat, heavy coat and fur lined gloves that had made the first portion of the trip bearable. She proceeded to tell me that she really liked me a lot and she thought we could have a future together if I were willing to become a Catholic. She went on to say she had gone to morning mass at church for the past nine days saying a prayer for my willingness to become a convert to her faith. This form of focused prayer is better known as a

Novena for a special intention. The last thing she did was hand me the prayer card she had elected to read for the past nine mornings with instructions to place the card in my pocket and read it before I went to bed that night

Her message to me was totally different from the words I had expected to hear. It had caught me totally off guard and seemed to imply a lifetime together which I had never seriously considered. I told her I thought I loved her, but could not give her a response that night. I promised her I would read the prayer and let her know my answer prior to the coming week-end which was our standard time for dates. I kissed her and was back out the door in far less time than my trip to the bus stop had taken.

I had to agree with her that this definitely was a serious talk and could only be handled by a face to face meeting. The problem was it left me more confused than ever. I desperately needed time for some serious reflection before we could have our next discussion. Thank God I had enough sense to tell her that before I left.

The brightly lit bus pulled up to its stop shortly after I arrived. I noticed the bus was sparsely populated as I climbed aboard. I took a seat on a side facing bench seat across the aisle from the rear passenger exit door. The few people riding home were all seated ahead of me. Most people seemed to be reading or resting, but the older couple closest to me seemed to be discussing the events of their day with one another.

    I was very curious about the prayer card and since no one was near me I decided this was as good a time as any to read that prayer for the first time. The card featured a depiction of Mary and is called the Memorare prayer. The words of that prayer follow:

Remember Oh most gracious Virgin Mary
That never was it known that
Anyone who fled to thy protection,
Implored thy help or
Sought thy intercession was left unaided
Inspired by this confidence, I fly onto you
Oh virgin of virgins, my mother.
To thee do I come. Before thee I stand,
Sinful and sorrowful.
Oh mother of the word incarnate
Despise not my petitions;
But in thy mercy, hear and answer me.
Amen.

I closed my eyes and began to think about the words I had just read and about my future. I knew that I wanted to be a high school teacher, but I was uncertain whether to pursue the field of instrumental music or biology which were worlds apart. Which path should I pursue? Which school should I attend? Where does Doris fit in the equation? Does God care which religion I choose?

I had attended church with her several different times and to be honest, I thought it strange that their mass was all in Latin with an English translation so that we would have some idea about what the priest was saying. I also thought the congregation left me confused as I was never certain what to do next as they sat, kneeled and stood at various times during the mass.

Suddenly, in the midst of all these chaotic thoughts, time seemed to stop. All conversations on the bus ceased and all sounds of traffic vanished from my mind. Then a profound and indescribable calm came over me. I felt, for the first and only time in my life, completely at peace. I now equate this peace to the peace Christ offered to His disciples when

He appeared to them in the upper room soon after His death. Then I heard ten words that changed my whole life. The voice sounded like a female voice which I was certain belonged to Mary. She was answering my prayer with the words **"Marry this girl. She will help you get to heaven."**

I opened my eyes fully expecting to see a vision of Mary along with the others on the bus. She was not there much to my surprise. The people were still reading or resting with the exception of the couple who were still talking quietly about their day. I could not understand why they were not all looking around in amazement searching for the source of that voice. Then it finally dawned on me. That voice had to be in my head. Either God sent Mary to answer my prayer or I was losing my mind. Which explanation was correct?

I don't remember anything else about that night including my walk home from the bus stop. I slept well without hearing any more voices and awoke the next morning certain God had answered all my questions. I would become a member of the Catholic Church. My career path would be science, my school would be Creighton University and Doris would be my wife. How could we fail? She and those ten words were my ultimate gifts from God. This mysterious event would be our secret for more than forty years.

I completed faith formation classes and became a Catholic right before Christmas of my sophomore year, became engaged during the spring of that same year and we were married on June 17, 1961 immediately after Doris had graduated from a three year program in medical Technology. We celebrated our fiftieth anniversary on June 17, 2011and are still happily married.

It would be almost fifty years after my experience for a neurobiologist to map the area in the brain that is activated during these experiences (see *"Soul Search"* Discover Magazine). This type of mysterious happening is identified as an inner locution and the area stimulated is at the junction between the temporal lobe involved in hearing and the parietal lobe where the speech center is located in our brains. Inner locutions rank next to apparitions as the most powerful influencers on faith formation and behavior modification within individuals who experience this phenomenon. It certainly influenced my own involvement within numerous parishes that we have attended as we moved from one place to another over the past fifty years. I have made it a point to play an active role in at least one church ministry for all but the first three years following our marriage. That pattern remains to this day. Perhaps I could have started earlier, but graduation, marriage and the arrival of the first two of our six children on top of my first teaching job kept me pretty busy. It was part of my vow I made to God in thanksgiving for His precious gift of love.

    I have said this prayer thousands of times since I first slipped that prayer card into my pocket and have never heard that voice again. God must have decided that one prayer so clearly answered should suffice. I have no earthly idea why God chose me to receive His grace in this way, but I will be forever grateful.

Questions:
I have shared this story many times now and continue to be amazed at how many have had

similar experiences. Have you had a similar experience?

If so, have you shared it with others or have you kept it a secret for fear that others might think you are crazy? Don't fear for this phenomenon is widespread throughout the world and is most likely to occur at the end of historical eras.

If you have not had a life changing experience, does this mean that God considers you less important to Him; or that He has a different role for you to play?

If your role is different, what might that role be?

7

How I Became the Absent Minded Professor

Tendencies tend to develop in a person over a prolonged period of time. One of the qualities common to professors is that they focus their attention on information in their field to the point that they tend to exclude everything else. I first became aware of this tendency in second or third grade.

One day my teacher told our class when we finished whatever assignment she had given us, to bring the paper up to her and then read some new information she had placed on her bulletin boards. I was one of the first to finish and started reading something that captured my imagination. Soon most of the students were standing around three big bulletin boards spread out around the classroom. Eventually she told us all to return to our seats, but I never heard her. Even worse, I never noticed that I was the only child not back at my desk. I was still reading something quite fascinating and was oblivious to the world around me. The mention of my name brought me back to the real world instantly, but it was too late. I knew I was in trouble when the teacher said "Billy, don't you think it would be nice if you followed directions like all your classmates?" All my peers found this hilarious and were laughing as I returned to my seat thoroughly embarrassed. I vowed that night to do all my serious reading and thinking at home. That tendency did not return to haunt me again until after I had completed my undergraduate degree.

    I was now the high school chemistry teacher at Bay View High School in Milwaukee, Wisconsin. We had one child and my wife was expecting another. We lived on the second floor of a large home which had a laundry room in the basement. Our typical after dinner routine started with Doris washing and my drying and putting away the dishes. Then I would take out the trash to an outside dumpster while she started getting our one year old ready for bed. It was a cold night so I put on my hat and coat and tied up our bag of trash for the dumpster. Doris asked me to bring up a laundry basket full of folded diapers when I returned. My directions were simple and so I started to think about how I was going to get my students to comprehend gas laws in class the next day as I started down the steps.

I was headed back up the steps a few minutes later when I realized I was supposed to be bringing something with me. I soon recalled that I had forgotten to pick up something in the laundry room so I reversed direction and continued down the second flight of stairs to the basement. I was immediately reminded of my mission when I spotted the basket of diapers as I glanced around the laundry room. I also spotted something out of the ordinary as well. I discovered the sealed bag of trash protruding from the top of the washing machine. I corrected my errors and proudly returned to the apartment with the folded diapers. Doris thought my outrageous behavior good enough to merit another long laugh when I shared the story with her later that night.

Those incidents became more frequent during the next four years. Finally, one night Doris found me staring blankly into an open refrigerator. She asked me what I was looking for and I told her I was searching for my red pen so that I could correct some biology exams. She suggested I close the refrigerator door and look for the red pen on or in my desk. Naturally, the red pen was on the desk right on top of the exams needing to be graded. My wife then announced that she had given up and that it was clearly time for me to become the absent minded professor as intended. I returned to school the next year on an NIH genetics training fellowship. I completed my PhD three years later with a focus upon DNA Replication and Repair. Now all I needed was a job at a college or university where my absent minded behavior would be less likely viewed as out of the ordinary.

Questions:
This story does not seem to have any connection to faith at first glance, but reveals an insight into who I really am. Our minds make us unique. The quirk just described in this chapter and my responses to experiences and events presented in other chapters makes me and all the other absent minded professors truly unique. You can ask a certain wonderful lady named Nancy back in Joplin, Missouri if my behavior was out of the ordinary. Nancy was

the secretary for all the professors in math and sciences at our school. My wife asked her how she communicated messages to all the professors one day. Nancy said "I look in their eyes and if they are with me, I give them the message. Otherwise, I wait until they come back to the real world."

What makes you unique?

Can you imagine how boring life would be if we were all identical with exactly the same life experiences to shape our faith?

How does the uniqueness of each individual mind influence who we are and what we do as well as the paths we take as we search for God?

8

Prayer Answered

I mentioned the circumstances that provided me the opportunity to complete my doctoral studies in the last chapter. I ended that chapter with a line stating all I needed was a job at a college or university. What I had failed to mention was that I already had a family consisting of a wife and four very young boys ranging in age from about one to six years old when I had arrived to begin this adventure. We were now all three years older and poorer and I was anxious to share my new found knowledge with college or university students.

I began to review the job opportunities advertised in the Chronicle of Higher Education at the beginning of my final year of study. I submitted applications and resumes to every college or university seeking entry level biology candidates. I even sent inquiry letters to several colleges and universities in our area that were not advertising positions. This translated into approximately eighty applications and fifty inquiries in total.

I was still looking for that elusive position after I completed a successful dissertation defense In July. Time was now growing short and we were beginning to feel desperate. None of my inquiries had even generated an interview.

There is a small recreational area within five miles of Manhattan, Kansas which natives of the area called Tuttle puddle. It was short for the Tuttle Creek Reservoir and Recreational Area. We had taken the boys to it on several occasions during the past three years. It was definitely one of their favorite sites for exploration. We would frolic on the beach and then we would begin our search for creatures or good skipping rocks to bounce across the generally smooth water. That day we played in the water for a while then told the boys they could wander along the shore on their own as long as they remained within sight of us.

Doris and I began a frantic discussion about how we were going to survive without a job just as soon as the boys were out of earshot. The discussion quickly dissolved into tears from both of us as we cried out to God for help. Then we devised a strategy that we would begin to enact on Monday. I had agreed that I would call my last employer to see if I might be able to resume teaching at the secondary level. I would then see if the latest issue of The Chronicle was advertising any new biology positions. It was very doubtful given the proximity of the date for fall classes to begin! We had also agreed that I would ask my advisor on Friday of the coming week if I might be able to remain there for another semester to continue a new research project that I had begun to pursue as soon as the dissertation had been completed. If none of these options worked out, Doris would see if she could move from a part time to a fulltime position in one of the hospital laboratories either in Manhattan or back in Omaha. Fortunately, none of those last second ideas ever had to proceed past the inquiry phase. I received two telephone calls within days of each other during the following week. I flew to Provo, Utah to interview for a microbiology position at Weber State College. Two days later I was in Joplin Missouri to interview for a position teaching microbiology and genetics at

Missouri Southern State College. Both schools offered me a full time teaching position. I accepted the Joplin school contract simply because it was a permanent position instead of a temporary slot.

I cannot begin to describe how relieved we were the day I signed that contract. Our frantic cry to God for help had been heard further strengthening the development of my faith. Classes began just two weeks later and I was never more excited. .

Questions:
What do you think? Was this an example of prayer answered or just dumb luck that I went from a person with no job prospects to one with two options to choose between in a matter of a week? I spent the last seventeen years of my career being the one placing those calls for interviews for openings within my division. In each instance the search committee poured over the applications of every qualified applicant. There was seldom very little to distinguish one applicant from another and the final candidates selected for interview often boiled down to the collective gut instinct of the

committee. Who really knows how a given candidate percolates to the top. Who is to say God was not playing a role as we sifted through the applicant pool searching for the best candidate. I certainly hope He was guiding us throughout the process. It is my observation that all selection committees wish to hire the best available candidate and I thank God our frantic prayers were heard.

Questions:
What are the strongest examples of prayer answered in your own life?
Do you agree that answered prayer is one of the easiest ways to strengthen faith?
What happens to a person's faith when prayers do not produce the desired result?
What are some of the reasons why prayer is not always answered?

9

Crisis

Some people reading to this point in the book might think that my story reads more like a fairy tale than one of a developing faith. They would be right in a way because every experience to this point has had a happy ending that seems pretty far removed from the real world many have encountered.

This story has a decidedly different ending. Oddly enough, this chapter of my life ultimately deepens my faith.

We moved to Joplin in August of 1971. I was very excited about my new position and the opportunity to utilize my newly acquired knowledge. Doris got a job as a hematologist at St John's Medical Center on the week-ends. We enrolled our three school age boys at St. Mary's Catholic grade School and our lives began to adjust to a new routine after the frenzy of the prior month.

The routine was short lived as Jimmy, our four year old, started taking naps in front of the television and waking up each afternoon with a temperature that would go away within a few hours. Doris knew immediately that something was seriously wrong with Jimmy, but I naively thought that everything was going to be alright as soon as whatever virus he had acquired ran its course.

The fever persisted for at least six more weeks in spite of trips to the doctor's office seeking a diagnosis. Doris' mom had come down to help with Jimmy and to spend Thanksgiving with us. Jimmy was admitted to St. Johns for further testing on the day after Thanksgiving of 1971. The hospital lab ran every test they could think of and I still remember the day when the lab manager, a new friend of ours, called and said the tests for leukemia, Rocky Mountain Spotted Fever, and Cat Scratch Fever had all come back negative.

Sadly, the health of Jimmy continued to decline. It was clear the doctors in Joplin did not have a diagnosis, so they helped Doris, her mom and Jimmy get space on a commercial flight back to Children's Hospital in Omaha on the Wednesday after Thanksgiving.

The people at Children's Hospital admitted Jimmy following the successful flight. I stayed home with the other three boys and tried to finish off my first semester of classes at MSSC. Doris and I were in daily communication about Jimmy's condition which was continuing to deteriorate. At least the doctors in Omaha had a suspicion about his illness and needed to perform a liver biopsy to confirm their suspicions. The procedure was risky and they thought that I should be present.

I drove up with the children that same day and Sam Gibson, my new department head, came along with me. I had left my grade book and all my final exams with others in the department who would monitor my exams in my absence. We took the boys to my mom and dad's house and then I rushed to the hospital.

I arrived and found a scared little boy who had no idea what was happening to him. The doctors sedated him within a few hours of my arrival to perform the biopsy. Jimmy went into a crisis following the procedure and immediately spiraled out of control toward death.

Doris spent every moment of the next two weeks at the hospital with him. She would hold him for hours at a time and read to him. She caught a few hours of sleep from time to time, but refused to go home. I would come to the hospital every day and try to relieve her, but she insisted that her place was at the hospital and that I should be the official communicator keeping our families informed of any changes in his condition.

It was now early in the morning of December 22. I met Doris down in Jimmy's room and we decided to go into the hospital chapel as we had done on several prior occasions. We prayed for a few moments and though I had stubbornly refused to admit that death was an outcome, I suddenly knew that death was inevitable. I guess I really knew that Jimmy was not going to make it when I looked in on him prior to our chapel visit and saw his unconscious little body sleeping in that big bed with all its tubes and monitors, but it did not hit me that this would be his final day on earth until I was praying at that moment.

We went back to the room to look in on him once more, and then Doris returned to her vigil while I came to tell our three boys and our parents that Jimmy wasn't coming home. He was going home to God instead.

After all our immediate family had been informed, I went back to the hospital. Jimmy died shortly after midnight on the morning of December 23.

Telling my three boys that Jimmy wasn't going to survive was the hardest thing I ever had to do in my life. In less than half a year I had gone from a person who was on top of the world to someone who suddenly realized that he never was in control of his destiny. I had studied DNA replication and repair which was the key to life and I was teaching courses in microbiology and genetics to college students, yet I did not know anything about a new disease called Lederer Siwe disease. I had never even heard of it. I now know that this disease which killed Jimmy is due to a virus that targets genetically predisposed individuals. It is very much like leukemia except that the cell that had become cancerous was a stationary macrophage fighting infection in the lymph nodes and thus not detectable in peripheral circulation.

I was certain that science had all the answers and hospitals cured illnesses rather than let their patients die. Man was I ever wrong!! I was furious with God! I blamed Him for turning what I had prayed would be a Merry Christmas into a crappy Christmas. I found that I could see only one positive throughout all this disaster. Doris was at my side as we emerged into a bitter and devastating early morning bringing this ugly episode to its crushing conclusion.

Questions:
Have you ever lost a child or known someone else who has experienced this particular type of loss?
How could you have intervened to ease their pain?
Can you ever imagine my guilt, my anger, my pain, and the sense of loss experienced by me at the conclusion of this crisis? Multiply this by 10 and it will give an impression of the devastation my wife felt.
I suspect that each of us has become angry at God over something at one time or another when the outcome prayed for did not

materialize. What triggered your anger and has the issue been resolved?

What is the worst crisis you have faced? Were your feelings similar to those for Doris and I?

I mentioned that this crisis oddly strengthened my faith. How could this be? Attempt to answer the question for yourself. My answer to this question may surprise you. It can be found on the last page of chapter 10 directly after the final chapter question.

10

The Importance of Relationships

"There is an appointed time for everything,…
A time to be born, and a time to die;…
A time to weep, and a time to laugh;
a time to mourn, and a time to dance….
A time to love, and a time to hate;
a time of war, and a time of peace."
(Taken from Ecclesiastes 3:1-8)

I have mentioned from the beginning of this book that God uses our relationships with people, places, objects and events to help Him build an everlasting relationship with us. The single most important relationship that any of us has is our relationship with God. Christ reaffirmed this point when He told us to love God with our whole heart and soul, but right at the moment when Jimmy died, our relationship with God was being severely tested. It felt to me like love for God was being replaced by hate and anger. We both hated that the son we loved so very much had been stripped from our lives and I, at least, took my anger out on God. I needed an answer to my biggest question at a minimum. Why take our son when there seems to be no shortage of neglected and unloved children in our world? I asked God that question repeatedly during the days and weeks following the funeral, but no answer was immediately forthcoming. Perhaps there is no acceptable answer when the parents are grieving and isolated from family and friends in a strange new place known as Joplin.

I give credit to Doris for keeping our daily routines including meals, hygiene, budget, mass obligations and faith in order during those early days following the death of Jimmy. She gives credit to me for being patient, understanding and a strong comforting presence to her and the family throughout our ordeal. It was the way we chose to express our love for one another, but both of us were hurting and my faith was shattered.

How did God respond to our needs? He sent four of His best couples to our rescue. I call them our pot-luck group. Each of these couples is so amazing that I need to pause here long enough to share some of the adversity they had to overcome in their own lives in order to become the successful faith filled people we came to know.

Gary, the youngest of four children, was abandoned by his father while he was still in the womb and lost much of his youth as he started working as a pin setter in a neighborhood bowling alley when he was only nine years old. Carole became a paraplegic when she was thrown from a car following a serious crash that left her with a broken back while she was still in college. The accident occurred just one month prior to her planned wedding. Her fiancé could not imagine life with a wheel chair bound wife and chose to cancel the wedding. Kent was blindsided by a careless driver and literally lost his whole family in an instant. His young wife and soon to be first born child died in the crash and he was seriously injured during that horrendous evening. His physical wounds healed up in time, but he could have been the poster boy for post-traumatic stress syndrome.

God rescued each of these individuals long before Doris and I ever knew them. There is absolutely nothing exaggerated in these three events. Each event could have destroyed a lesser individual. What pulled them from the depths of their despair? Each of these individuals say God sent them an extraordinary person that made their lives complete. God brought a faith filled angel named Carole Lou into Gary's life and they were married a year later. Both would agree that their undying love for each other, their four children and their eight grandchildren is the driving force in their lives. Charlie is the knight in shining armor who rescued Carole, his damsel in distress. He took one look at her and knew that this was the person God intended for him. They have been married for 56 years now and Carole bore four children who produced ten loving grandchildren who add so much joy to their lives. Kent was an optometrist. He was knocked off his feet by a marvelous young lady who brought her mother into the office for a routine eye exam. He asked the daughter, a young lady named Marilyn, for a date on the spot. Marilyn's father was very concerned about this brash young man, but the date was meant to be. It was the first date for Kent since the fatal car crash, but must have been magic for they were engaged one week later. He was baptized into her church on her birthday and married the following month during the Thanksgiving week-end. Both have given thanks to God ever since the moment they first met. They have two married children and are so proud of their only grandson.

The last couple in our group was Lou and Sandy. Neither of them appeared to have experienced any obstacles in their lives as they seemed happily married with three beautiful young children. We quickly learned that everyone Lou met was his friend. No one was a stranger for more than a few minutes as he was full of life and love for others. I thought of him as a modern day Good Samaritan. Then, one day, Lou was emotionally crushed when his wife suddenly left him for another man.

Our group was in shock. How could such a thing happen to such a good man? Lou would freely admit that he was lost for a time and even felt somewhat uncomfortable as the only single parent in our group. He ultimately met another lady named Jo, with a heart as big as his. They welcomed each other's large families as if they were their own children and soon were married.

We hardly knew any of these couples prior to the death of Jimmy, but they showered us with a love that sustained us. We bonded during that time and have stayed close for more than forty years now. This was no small feat as we and one other couple moved to distant cities and the three remaining couples stayed in the Joplin area; and although not hurt, lost much of their homes in the tornado that devastated Joplin in 2011.

What did these couples teach me about God? They showed me by example that God loves all of His creation including us and that God is not the cause of the crises that every living person encounters at various times in his/her life. They taught us that there is a time to be born and a time to die and that the God who loves us uses these moments of adversity to help us grow in faith. The first three individuals I introduced in this chapter are great examples of this truth. All three became converts to Catholicism and have been active in their church from the moment they met their spouse.

They taught our whole family that it was time to stop weeping and mourning and to begin laughing and playing again. We made it a point to eat, play and laugh together at least once or twice a month for the next twelve years. Then we moved to Florida and our potluck nights turned into annual week long reunions at various places all around this great country.

They taught us we are called to love one another as Christ commanded and the best time to share that love is when others are in need. Christians consider adversity as the crosses they must carry as they journey on their path to Christ. The love they showered upon us in our hour of need made our first big cross much lighter.

At some point I realized that it was time to stop my stupid war with God and to begin making peace. Once I took this step, I finally realized that I had not lost a son, but gained my very own saint. Then when Jo's son was killed in an accident, I realized that it was now my turn to start returning that love in their hour of need.

Our association with these couples with their positive outlook definitely helped us emerge from our first big crisis as a better couple. Many other family and friends have been present to help when other crises have arisen. I cherish all these Relationships established over the years.

Questions:
Who are the individuals you turn to when you encounter a crisis that is just too big to handle alone?
Do they pull you back to the positive end of the pendulum like our pot-luck group did? It is the only way Doris and I found for escape from despair.
Who are the individuals you have reached out to in their hour of need? This is a huge part of our mission during the brief time we remain on earth.

I consider this the single most important chapter in this book because it tells us what I believe to be the most important reason why God tries to establish a relationship with us. He needs us to "love one another as I have loved you". It is why every single religion includes the Golden Rule. Who are the others that you love?

Has your love for them remained strong or is there some issue that needs to be forgiven and forgotten so that love can be refreshed?

Does your love extend beyond your immediate family? If not, what more could you do to begin making a difference within your community?

How does the death of my child strengthen my faith?

It took me three long years to come to terms with the death of Jimmy. I transitioned from an angry person to one accepting God as infinitely more wise and loving than I would ever be. My transition began when I finally realized we are born imperfect and placed into an imperfect world. The genetic imperfection in Jimmy was more than he could overcome. While death was the outcome, it was not the end; God simply brought him home earlier than I was ready to accept.

This was the first cross I had been asked to bear. I came through this crisis stronger than ever thanks, in part, to these wonderful couples. These couples acted as the good Samaritans, making our cross much lighter.

God knew that I could handle this cross, but Doris could not without His assistance. God paved the way for this crisis by giving her extra sensory perception (ESP) during this critical period. It began when her mother, who called about once a month, phoned one evening while we were finishing dinner. Doris said as she got up to answer the phone "This is weird. That's my mom on the line and she is calling to tell me that my uncle is ill and in the hospital." The words she spoke were confirmed as she picked up the phone. This was her first ESP experience.

The ESP continued through the death of Jimmy and the death of her father. Each time she knew the purpose and outcome of the event prior to its happening. She knew Jimmy was dying before I even knew he was sick thanks to her ESP.

She mentioned sometime after her father's funeral that while she hated the ESP because everything she knew about was bad, she was certain the ESP was God's way of helping her cope with these events. When I heard these words for the first time, my tenuous peace treaty with God became permanent helping me through the other crises in my life.

11

A Close Call

Jesus calls us in many ways. My call was most unusual. I did not fully recognize it until I experienced the events reported in this chapter. It truly was my wake up call.

This story began with a trip to the hospital to replace a defective heart valve. I accepted this was a major surgery, but never imagined that I might be one of the four percent to experience complications. I had a great surgeon who specialized in heart valve replacement. I was reasonably young, just sixty, and considered myself to be in excellent health other than the defective heart valve. I fully expected to be back on my feet and ready to resume my career as an academic administrator at the local community college at the beginning of the next semester. I had even arranged my surgery for the week before Thanksgiving in order to utilize the Thanksgiving and Christmas breaks for rehabilitation.

The initial open heart surgery appeared to go quite well and I was released from the hospital on the day before Thanksgiving. I went back to the local emergency room knowing something was wrong the following day. I believe I must have passed out about the time I was wheeled through the emergency room doors and remember almost nothing about the next month. I was told I experienced cardiac arrest while in intensive care prior to my cardiologist visiting the next morning and was flown back to the hospital where my original surgery had been performed once I was stable enough for transport.

Several weeks later I struggled awake to the sound of my name. At least I thought I had heard my name, but the voice sounded faint and quite far away. Perhaps this was just my imagination at work. No! There it was again. It was more distinct and urgent this time – "Bill. Come on Bill. I know you can do it. Push. You must try harder Bill – just push".

I opened my eyes and saw myself for the first time. As I looked down upon myself, I saw that I was lying in a box that had been placed upon a stainless steel table. That box reminded me of a very plain coffin. It was painted a dull medium gray color and was completely devoid of any ornamentation. The lid was divided into two halves with the bottom half closed so that I could only see the top portion of my body. The other half of the lid was open and appeared to be made from a dark smoky gray piece of opaque plastic or glass.

My first thought was that I was in the cheapest casket I had ever seen. I blinked hard and tried to make sense of what was happening. This time when I opened my eyes I was still inside the box, but the lid seemed to be directly in front of my face. What had the unfamiliar voice asked me to do? She had asked me to push. The only thing my drugged mind could think to do was to try and push that piece of plastic or glass away from my face. I was amazed at the apparent weight pressing down around me, but I pushed with all my might and slowly the lid began to rise. At least my right hand felt the lid begin to swing open. (I now believe that female voice belonged to a nurse who had asked me to move one of my fingers or toes in response to some stimulus. The words I heard were her way of arousing me from my coma.)

Now I could hear several voices around me as my mind madly searched for an understanding of what was happening. At last I heard the voice of my wife, Doris, who had been at my side for most of my life. She was standing there again and holding my hand. She explained that I had been in a coma for the last three weeks and that I was finally back in the land of the living.

I definitely had experienced my own version of a close encounter with death. I began to learn just how close during my next few weeks in intensive care. My wife and nurses immediately told me something I already knew. I did not need them to inform me that I was blind. I could not even distinguish light from dark

I spent the next three weeks in intensive care. During that time I learned that my body had been subjected to a second round of open heart surgery to correct a leak that was filling my pericardial sac with blood. They referred to this complication as tamponade. I also went through a couple of rounds of abdominal surgery to reduce abdominal swelling prior to being in a medically induced coma. They described the abdominal condition as compartment syndrome. The hope was that my body would recover from these frontal assaults. It did, thanks to the prayers of family and friends.

I did awaken only to discover everything else that had gone wrong. My wife and nurses informed me my electrolytes were way out of balance, I was in acute renal failure, and my blood chemistry profile also indicated I was in acute liver failure.

There really are few entertainment options when bedridden. The activities are further reduced when blindness is part of the equation and the location is labeled intensive care. TV watching and monitor watching are lost options. That is too bad as I am hooked up to lots of interesting monitors. Maybe my mind could no longer receive visual signals, but it had plenty of time to think. I used this time to review the circumstances surrounding my return to the land of the living.

I had read about others who had near death experiences. They describe a bright light which most individuals associate with God. Since I had not seen a bright light I tended to believe I was one of the unfortunate many who come close to death without experiencing God. Then it dawned on me. Many scientists had assumed the reported light may have been one of the many strong beams used in the operating room to illuminate the patient undergoing surgery. Perhaps the absence of light was a product of my blindness.

A second point of departure from those who claim to have had a close encounter with death was also missing. I did not experience seeing major events of my life flash by.

I did have the experience of floating above my body and seeing it in what I thought of as a gray casket. This is better known as an out of body experience. I felt very calm as I looked down upon myself.

I guess it really does not matter what I had experienced. I knew in my heart that I had been spared. Perhaps I did have most of my organ systems working poorly or not at all. Perhaps the blindness would be with me for the rest of my life, but I was alive.

I regained all of my functions with the exception of sight during my next few weeks in intensive care. My world was just as dark as the first day when I knew I was blind, but at long last I was going home. I was a survivor, but why had God chosen to save me?

Questions:
Do you think that God really saves anyone?
Have you or anyone you have been close to ever had a near death experience? It seems to be a fairly common occurrence.
If you or someone you know has had a near death experience, describe this experience to your family. It will help them grow in faith while strengthening your own faith.

12

Putting It All Together

My close call with death, described in the previous chapter, left me with a severe case of survivor's guilt. It also left me changed in two fundamental ways. I was no longer afraid of death and I was now more certain God had something important for me to do before I checked out for good. While I did not know what He had planned for me, I was certain reading and prayer would help me put it all together. <u>Wisdom of the Ages</u> an inspirational Wayne Dyer tape given to me by one of my daughters- in- law and <u>The Purpose Driven Life</u> by Rick Warren began to point me in the right direction.

Wayne Dyer told of the sixty most influential individuals in the history of mankind. Each of them was chosen because they were powerful communicators whose ideas helped transform minds. Wayne Dyer also challenged the reader to organize his or her thoughts and then get up the courage to share those thoughts with others.

Rick Warren said that God never makes junk and that each person created by God has a purpose. He also indicated that our purpose changes throughout life.

Older persons often sense that they have no purpose once their children are raised.

I placed myself in this group and was content to sit back and let the world go by without much thought until I experienced my close call with death. When I awoke from my coma, each day was viewed as a gift from God and never to be wasted. I was much more sensitive as a person. I became more attuned to the needs and concerns of others. Patriotic and religious messages as well as great music frequently left me in tears.

I also felt guilty about not sharing more about my unique gift of faith with others. Perhaps it was now time to turn that around.

The clincher came one Sunday morning while listening to a Gospel reading on the parable of the talents (Mathew 25:14-30). This parable tells of three servants who have been given one or more gold coins (talents) from their master. The first two servants double their investments which pleases the master.

The third servant takes his single talent and buries it. Years later he digs it up and gives it back to the master when He returns. The master (God) is angry because no one has benefitted from the gift.

I suddenly realized as I sat there in church that I was just like that timid little man. I had been given my own special talent and buried it so deep that the gift profited no one else. The gift was my Message from Mary which left me with a faith so strong that I have served in many church ministries spread over seven parishes for more than forty eight consecutive years now. Yet I had buried those ten little words so deep that even my own children were unaware of my message from Mary. I could not explain the origin of the voice I heard so many years ago or prove as a scientist that God existed, so I said nothing. Comments made about my schizophrenic uncle labeling him as a crazy God freak, contributed to my own decision to remain silent. I really thought others would think of me as another crazy little man who heard voices.

My close call with death had given me a reprieve. The two books just mentioned encouraged me to seek a new purpose and strengthened my resolve to shout that message out to anyone willing to listen.

The outcome of all this is that I began by sharing my faith with my own immediate family and then with numerous friends and small faith communities ranging from lay led retreats to potential new RCIA members within our church. This book is another way for me to expand my outreach to others.

Why would I do such a thing? The most straight forward answer is that I believe with my whole heart that God has given me a second chance to invest that single talent He gave me one night long ago when riding home on a bus.

It is now time to help you put thoughts about your own faith together. Hopefully, you discovered this message to be inspirational. If so, it helped erase your own doubt about the existence of God and reconfirmed or strengthened your faith. That was my primary objective and would be a satisfactory result. Answering the questions at the end of each chapter would enhance the outcome because they help you to focus upon experiences and events in your own faith journey. These events and experiences are personal and much more satisfying because they help the individual discover the steps God took in His desire to build relationships with all of us. I believe you would be amazed if you began to write those ideas down. Writing helps to solidify random thoughts into meaningful ideas which are so much more powerful in transforming or enhancing your own faith life. Now I would ask you to go one additional step. Print them out and share them with your own family and friends.

Why would I ask you to do this? I mentioned at the beginning of this chapter that God never makes junk. That message is vitally important to everyone reading this book. The creation of every human life is a miraculous event made more meaningful because He made you for a reason. That reason is to bloom and grow wherever you are planted.

Think about the varieties of flowers that you have encountered all over our planet. Think of the size and coloration of the blooms. Think of their scents or odors. Think of their shapes that range from simple to complex designs, yet all flowers play the same role; they insure survival of their species from generation to generation. They are different from one another just like us and it is our differences that make us unique and give us our purpose.

While we all are different, we all have the same basic needs. We need nourishment of mind, body and soul. We need shelter and security, but most of all we need love.

We live in an increasingly secular society with many who have lost sight of God. A select few representing a very small minority would like to transform our God fearing nation into a Godless country. They are taking advantage of our complacency.

I am all in favor of our nation remaining as one nation, <u>under God</u>, indivisible with liberty and justice for all as intended by our forefathers. I am certain all readers share this view. The question is how do we move the focus of our nation back to God who was so important at its founding?

My story won't turn this picture around, but if I could get a thousand people to tell their personal experiences of the presence of God in their own lives with their children, we could begin to make a difference.

Questions:

Think back to the parable of the talents mentioned in this chapter and the parable of the workers in the vineyard where God rewarded the individuals hired in the afternoon at the same daily rate as those who began their workdays in the morning or at noon. Do both of these parables suggest that God views each individual equally important as long as each strives to make a difference?

Why does God wish us all to be more like little children?

Did you rediscover that God has been seeking you on various occasions in your own faith journey?

What were those occasions and have you shared them with others?

If you are not satisfied with your own faith at this point, what are some of the things you can do to strengthen that faith?

Do you compare yourself to the person with ten or a hundred talents and thus conclude that your life is unimportant to God? All He asks is that we like the smallest of flowers, bloom and grow where we are planted. By doing this, we let His image shine in our world. May God fill our hearts with joy as we strive to make a difference!

Conclusion

There are many paths leading to God. My most recent path has caused me to reexamine and ultimately to write about the development of my own faith. It identifies both the current path I am travelling and what I am doing to fulfill my most recent purpose.

I laid out an action plan for readers who find themselves on paths similar to my own in the last chapter. It is now time to consider action plans for those who find themselves on different paths or would never consider writing about God's role in their own life.

Each person is at a different developmental stage and on his/her own unique path toward God. It is what we do while on our paths that determines our destiny. I find it amazing that it is never too late to make amends when we find ourselves on the wrong path or choosing the wrong actions. The next story validates this point quite clearly.

A long time ago there were three very bad men. They had committed many crimes prior to getting caught. In each instance they were found guilty and sentenced to death by the judge.

The night before their sentences were to be carried out, a fourth man was captured and brought before the judge with the demand that he be executed along with the other three. Since the captors were highly respected men in town, the judge agreed to hear the case. He listened to the testimony of the fourth man and quickly found the person innocent of any crime. He then proceeded to recommend the case be thrown out of court.

The man's accusers vehemently disagreed with the finding. They simply reiterated their demand for execution of the fourth man.

By now most readers are probably wondering just how this story has any relevance for them. Perhaps it would help if a few more details were provided. The judge was Pilot, the fourth man was Jesus, and His accusers were the chief priests and rabbis whose power base was being threatened. All Christians know the outcome of this story. One of the prisoners named Barabbas who had been found guilty of insurrection and murder was ultimately released and an innocent man named Jesus along with the two remaining prisoners was crucified.

We assume the two criminals crucified with Jesus must have committed more violent crimes than those of Barabbas since the crowd as well as the chief priests and rabbis preferred the release of Barabbas. Yet the responses of the two hardened criminals crucified with Jesus were dramatically different from one another as reported in chapter 23 of the Gospel of Luke.

Let me describe the reactions of the two thieves within the context of the rest of my story. Each thief is at the final fork in the road of life. Both are hanging on their crosses on either side of Jesus. The bad thief chooses to stay on the familiar road he has travelled throughout most of his life. We know this because he places his faith totally in himself playing the macho man, tough guy right up to the end. He first throws insults at Christ then joins with the crowd of onlookers mocking Jesus by shouting at Him to save Himself and save them as well.

The good thief chooses to depart from his sinful past by choosing the road less travelled.

He first takes stock of the life he has chosen to lead, realizes he has made some terrible choices and deserves his fate. We know this by the words he spoke while on his cross. We are told by Luke he first rebuked the other thief explaining that we were guilty and our sentence was just (a type of confession), but this man you mock has committed no sin and does not deserve this sentence. Then he humbly asks Jesus to "remember me when You come into Your kingdom."

Jesus chose to say nothing to the bad thief, but His reply to the good thief was simple and reassuring. "I tell you the truth. Today you will be with me in paradise." While we know these words were directed to the good thief, this last teaching message given by Jesus was also intended for us. God gave the good thief his one talent when He gave him life and he gave him one more opportunity to take the road less travelled by bringing him face to face with His Son.

If God could love the good thief, He most certainly loves us. All we have to do is love one another as He has loved us. We do this by striving to make a positive difference in the lives of the people around us. This could be as simple as putting a smile on the face of the lonely person next door, working in a food kitchen or thrift store, buying a gift for a poor child, saying a prayer for the stranger in need or any of countless other acts of charity and kindness bringing peace and joy to others.

We all have been given a most precious gift known as life. Each new day gives us another opportunity to take one more step toward or away from our Creator. What are you going to do each day to brighten or improve the lives of others? Whatever you propose becomes your purpose. Our acts of love convert it to an action plan. Your action plan can and will change throughout your life, but your actions, like those of the good Samaritan or even the good thief, have the potential to endear you to God's people and thus endear you to god. Just seek him and you shall find him in the events of your own time.

Questions:
What is your purpose at this point in your life?
What actions are you taking to give meaning to your purpose?

For Further Reading

The Shack by William P. Young for a contemporary look at the trinity or the three faces of God.

The Five People You Meet in Heaven by Mitch Albom is a great story extolling the virtues of an ordinary little man who finds himself in heaven.

The Greatest Miracle by Og Mandino describes beautifully how each of us is so miraculously made.

Wisdom of the Ages by Wayne Dyer was the first book I read which encouraged me to consider writing.

More than a Carpenter by Josh McDowell is one of many excellent books written about the life of Christ

<u>The Purpose Driven Life</u> by Rick Warren played a prominent role as I wrote portions of this book.

<u>The Day Will Come</u> by Michael H. Brown provides far more information about the mystical events associated with Mary known as apparitions and innerlocutions.

DVD by Dean Jones <u>St. John in Exile</u>. A powerful dramatic presentation reflecting the faith of the first Christians in the face of persecution.

"Soul Search" Discover magazine June 2007 for details of location of the portion of the brain activated when innerlocutions are heard.

Acknowledgements

Where does a person begin when it is time to recognize those who helped to shape me into the person that I am today? It begins with parents who loved each other and wanted to provide a secure environment for the growth of my brother and me. Their role was elucidated in the early chapters of my faith journey along with the contributions of my only nearby grandparent.

This book is dedicated to Doris, my wife. I would not have had a faith story worthy of publication without her Novena and prayer card to take my faith to a whole new level. She has proofed every chapter cleaning up the many spelling grammatical and spacing errors that were originally present in the manuscript. She also served as my technical director readying the book for publication. This translated into page layout and chapter formatting details that are far beyond my technical ability. She has been at my side for over fifty years helping to make me a better person. Thank you, sweetheart!

I have been blessed with a wonderful family who give me many reasons to be proud. All five children and their spouses have a college education and are making a positive difference in our world. They are also molding twelve wonderful grandchildren which are becoming a responsible new generation with strong moral values. Thank you children, spouses and grandchildren for contributing so much to my positive outlook on life!

Countless other friendships forged during my days at Adams and then at Benson, especially within the band, gave me confidence needed to proceed. New friendships were formed at every new academic destination and within every faith group encountered in my faith journey. You know who you are because we have maintained a long term and loving friendship over many years. My thanks go out to the pot luck group who made sure I got their stories straight and all the other friends we have stayed in contact with throughout the years. Each of you along with the many priests encountered along the way has helped to shape my faith.

I especially need to thank Craig and Gloria, Mike and Geri, Dave and Candy along with Father Fred Ruse who showed us the true meaning of love as our pastoral leader of our lay retreat ministry. It was your encouragement that led me to share parts of my story for the first time. I also thank Marilyn for providing me the opportunity to present some of my faith stories within RCIA during the past three years and to Mike and Arnie for giving me an opportunity to bounce some ideas around as this story began to take shape.

The writers Club under the leadership of Rosie and Bob helped me fine tune several of the chapters. The excellent critiques by Cheryl and Chris as they reviewed the manuscript resulted in a more professional and polished appearance to the final draft making it a much better reading book. Thank you one and all.

They say that a picture is worth a thousand words. That is an understatement when the picture serves as a book cover. It plays a major promotional role in book sales. I am proud to say my son, Bob designed the cover. His current entrepreneurial venture is better known as Tangerine Creative. This is his second cover design for me as he created the cover for <u>Better Dead than Bread</u> , a fictional book, which is currently available through Amazon.com.

www.ingramcontent.com/pod-product-compliance
Lightning Source LLC
Chambersburg PA
CBHW071307040426
42444CB00009B/1902